HUMAN SEX TRAFFICKING

TABLE OF CONTENTS

INTRODUCTION

In recent years, the healthcare system has become increasingly recognized as a critical frontline in the fight against human sex trafficking. This illicit and heinous crime affects countless individuals globally, often hidden in plain sight. Healthcare providers, due to their unique and regular interaction with a wide range of individuals, play a pivotal role in identifying and assisting victims. "Empowering Healthcare Providers: A Comprehensive Guide to Identifying and Addressing Human Sex Trafficking" is designed to equip healthcare professionals with the knowledge and skills necessary to combat this pervasive issue.

Human sex trafficking is a grave violation of human rights, where individuals are coerced or deceived into engaging in sex acts under duress. This crime transcends geographical, socio-economic, and cultural boundaries, impacting individuals from all walks of life. Traffickers exploit vulnerabilities such as poverty, lack of education, and social isolation, often subjecting victims to severe physical and psychological harm. For healthcare providers, recognizing and responding to the signs of trafficking is not just a matter of professional duty but a moral imperative.

This book is a call to action for healthcare providers to become active participants in the fight against human sex trafficking. By gaining a deeper understanding of this issue and applying the knowledge and strategies outlined in this guide, healthcare professionals can make a significant difference in the lives of trafficking survivors and contribute to the broader effort to eradicate this atrocity.

MODULE ONE

LESSON ONE: UNDERSTANDING HUMAN SEX TRAFFICKING

Human sex trafficking is a global crisis that affects millions of individuals annually, often hidden in plain sight. Understanding the definitions, scope, and impact of this heinous crime is crucial for healthcare providers to effectively recognize and support victims. This lesson provides a comprehensive overview of human sex trafficking, examining its various forms, the factors that facilitate its prevalence, and its profound effects on individuals and society.

Definitions and Key Concepts

Human sex trafficking, also known as sex trafficking, involves the exploitation of individuals through coercion, deception, or force for the purpose of commercial sex. The U.S. Department of State defines sex trafficking as a crime where individuals are recruited, enticed, or coerced into engaging in sexual acts through force, fraud, or coercion, and where the trafficker benefits from the exploitation.

Several key terms are important in understanding sex trafficking:

- Trafficking Victim: An individual who has been subjected to sex trafficking. Victims are often manipulated or controlled by traffickers and may experience severe trauma.
- Trafficker: The individual or group responsible for the exploitation of trafficking victims. Traffickers often use psychological manipulation, physical violence, or economic coercion to control their victims.

- Exploitation: The use of individuals for sexual activities for financial gain, often involving severe abuse and deprivation of autonomy.

Forms of Human Sex Trafficking

Human sex trafficking manifests in various forms, each with distinct characteristics:

- Street Prostitution: Victims are often forced to work on the streets or in public places, where they are vulnerable to arrest, abuse, and exploitation.
- Escort Services: Victims may be coerced into working for escort services, where they are marketed as "companions" but are exploited for sex.
- Brothels: Some trafficking victims are forced to work in brothels or illicit massage parlors, where they are controlled by traffickers and subjected to ongoing abuse.
- Online Exploitation: The internet has become a platform for traffickers to exploit victims through online advertising and illicit activities, such as live-streamed sex shows.

Scope and Prevalence

Human sex trafficking is a pervasive issue affecting countries worldwide. The scope of the problem is challenging to quantify due to its clandestine nature, but estimates suggest that millions of individuals are trafficked globally each year. The United Nations Office on Drugs and Crime (UNODC) reports that sex trafficking accounts for a significant portion of human trafficking cases, with women and children being disproportionately affected.

In the United States, the National Human Trafficking Hotline provides data on reported cases of trafficking, highlighting that sex trafficking is a major concern. Victims often come from diverse backgrounds, and traffickers exploit various vulnerabilities, including poverty, immigration status, and lack of education.

Impact on Victims

The impact of sex trafficking on victims is profound and multifaceted:

- Physical Health: Victims often endure severe physical abuse, including injuries from violence and neglect of medical care. They may also suffer from sexually transmitted infections (STIs) and unwanted pregnancies.
- Psychological Trauma: The psychological impact of trafficking is severe, with victims experiencing symptoms of post-traumatic stress disorder (PTSD), depression, anxiety, and dissociation. The trauma often results from both the abuse endured and the manipulative control exercised by traffickers.
- Social and Economic Effects: Victims may face social isolation, stigma, and economic exploitation. The trauma and abuse can hinder their ability to reintegrate into society, affecting their employment prospects and personal relationships.

Understanding human sex trafficking is the first step for healthcare providers in addressing this critical issue. By grasping the definitions, recognizing the various forms of trafficking, and acknowledging the widespread impact on victims, healthcare professionals can better identify and assist those affected.

MODULE TWO

LESSON ONE: RECOGNIZING THE SIGNS: IDENTIFYING VICTIMS OF HUMAN SEX TRAFFICKING IN HEALTHCARE SETTINGS

The ability to recognize victims of human sex trafficking within healthcare settings is a critical skill for medical professionals. Trafficking victims often present with a range of physical and psychological symptoms that can be misattributed to other conditions. This lesson focuses on how healthcare providers can identify potential trafficking victims by understanding key indicators and signs, as well as by utilizing effective assessment techniques. Early detection and intervention can significantly impact the well-being of trafficking survivors and aid in their recovery.

Physical Indicators

Victims of sex trafficking may exhibit various physical signs that suggest abuse or exploitation. These indicators include:

- Unexplained Injuries: Victims may have frequent, unexplained injuries such as bruises, lacerations, or fractures. These injuries may be in various stages of healing, indicating ongoing abuse.
- Sexually Transmitted Infections (STIs): The presence of STIs or recurrent infections may suggest that the individual is involved in sexual activities under duress. Multiple or unusual infections can be a red flag for trafficking.

- Neglect and Poor Hygiene: Victims may appear malnourished, unkempt, or show signs of neglect. Poor hygiene and untreated medical conditions can indicate a lack of proper care and supervision.
- Dental Issues: Dental problems, such as missing or damaged teeth, can result from physical abuse or poor access to dental care.

Behavioral Indicators

Behavioral signs can provide critical clues that someone might be a trafficking victim. These include:

- Fearful or Anxious Behavior: Victims may exhibit signs of extreme fear or anxiety, especially when questioned about their background or when they are separated from their companion. They may also appear overly compliant or submissive.
- Inconsistent Stories: Victims often provide inconsistent or vague details about their personal history or living conditions. Their stories may change frequently or lack coherence.
- Controlled Communication: If a victim is accompanied by someone who appears to be controlling their communication or responses, this may indicate trafficking. Victims may be reluctant to speak freely or may avoid eye contact.
- Fear of Authorities: Trafficking victims may show an intense fear of law enforcement or other authority figures due to previous negative experiences or threats from their traffickers.

Psychological Indicators

The psychological impact of trafficking can manifest in various ways, including:

- Post-Traumatic Stress Disorder (PTSD): Symptoms of PTSD, such as flashbacks, nightmares, or severe anxiety, are common among trafficking survivors. Victims may also exhibit signs of depression, dissociation, or emotional numbness.
- Low Self-Esteem and Self-Harm: Victims may display low self-esteem, self-hatred, or engage in self-harming behaviors. They might feel unworthy or undeserving of help due to the trauma they have experienced.
- Substance Abuse: The use of drugs or alcohol as a coping mechanism can be prevalent among trafficking survivors. Substance abuse may be used to numb emotional pain or as a tool for control by traffickers.

Social Indicators

Several social factors may also indicate that someone is a trafficking victim:

- Lack of Personal Identification: Victims often lack personal identification documents, such as a driver's license or passport. This lack of documentation can be a method of control used by traffickers.
- Isolation from Support Systems: Victims may be isolated from family and friends, and may not have access to a support network. They might be cut off from external social connections and resources.
- Frequent Relocations: Trafficking victims might have a history of frequent relocations or a lack of a permanent address, which can be a sign of efforts to evade detection by authorities.

Assessment Techniques

Effective assessment techniques can enhance the identification of trafficking victims:

- Confidential and Compassionate Interviews: Conducting interviews in a private, compassionate, and non-judgmental manner helps victims feel safe to disclose their situation. Building rapport and ensuring confidentiality are crucial for encouraging victims to speak openly.
- Using Screening Tools: Implementing standardized screening tools designed to identify trafficking indicators can be useful. These tools can help structure the assessment process and ensure that critical signs are not overlooked.
- Observing Interactions: Pay attention to interactions between the patient and their companions. Controlling or overly protective behavior from accompanying individuals can be a significant red flag.
- Training and Continuing Education: Ongoing training for healthcare providers is essential for staying updated on the latest indicators and best practices for identifying trafficking victims. Regularly reviewing case studies and emerging trends can improve recognition skills.

Case Examples

To illustrate these indicators in practice, consider the following examples:

Case Example 1: A young woman presents with multiple bruises and an untreated STI. During the interview, she is accompanied by a controlling male who answers questions for her and becomes defensive when asked about her background. The woman appears anxious and reluctant to speak.

Case Example 2: An adolescent girl visits a clinic with severe dental issues and signs of malnutrition. She provides inconsistent information about her living situation and avoids direct eye contact. She is isolated from friends and family and lacks personal identification.

Recognizing the signs of human sex trafficking within healthcare settings requires a keen eye and a compassionate approach. By understanding the physical, behavioral, psychological, and social indicators of trafficking, healthcare providers can better identify and assist victims. Effective assessment techniques, coupled with ongoing training and awareness, play a vital role in improving the identification process and ultimately supporting survivors in their path to recovery.

MODULE THREE

LESSON ONE: MEDICAL AND PSYCHOLOGICAL TRAUMA: ADDRESSING THE NEEDS OF TRAFFICKING SURVIVORS

Victims of human sex trafficking experience profound medical and psychological trauma due to the abuse and exploitation they endure. Addressing these needs effectively requires a comprehensive understanding of the unique health challenges faced by trafficking survivors. This lesson explores the medical and psychological impacts of trafficking and provides guidance on how healthcare providers can offer appropriate care and support.

Medical Trauma

Trafficking victims often face a range of medical issues resulting from their exploitation:

- Physical Injuries: Victims may present with a variety of physical injuries, including bruises, fractures, lacerations, and internal injuries. These injuries can result from violence inflicted by traffickers or from unsafe working conditions. Thorough medical examinations are essential to assess and treat these injuries.
- Sexually Transmitted Infections (STIs): The prevalence of STIs is high among trafficking survivors due to the nature of their exploitation. Common STIs include chlamydia, gonorrhea, syphilis, and human papillomavirus (HPV). Regular screening and appropriate treatment are crucial,

and healthcare providers should offer STI testing in a non-judgmental and supportive manner.

- Chronic Health Conditions: Trafficking survivors may suffer from chronic health conditions such as respiratory infections, gastrointestinal issues, or chronic pain resulting from neglect and poor living conditions. Comprehensive medical evaluations are necessary to diagnose and manage these conditions.

- Pregnancy and Reproductive Health: Victims may face unintended pregnancies and reproductive health issues. Providing access to prenatal care, reproductive health counseling, and options for pregnancy management (including termination if desired) is important for addressing these needs.

- Nutritional Deficiencies: Malnutrition and vitamin deficiencies are common among trafficking survivors due to inadequate food and poor living conditions. Healthcare providers should assess nutritional status and provide appropriate dietary recommendations or supplementation.

Psychological Trauma

The psychological impact of trafficking is severe and can include:

- Post-Traumatic Stress Disorder (PTSD): PTSD is a common condition among trafficking survivors. Symptoms may include flashbacks, nightmares, severe anxiety, and avoidance behavior. Trauma-informed care is essential in addressing PTSD, which involves creating a safe and supportive environment and employing therapeutic techniques such as cognitive-behavioral therapy (CBT).

- Depression and Anxiety: Depression and anxiety are prevalent among trafficking survivors due to the trauma they have experienced. Symptoms can range from persistent sadness and hopelessness to panic attacks and generalized anxiety. Providing mental health support through counseling and medication management is crucial for recovery.

- Dissociation and Emotional Numbness: Victims may experience dissociation, which involves feeling detached from reality or experiencing gaps in memory. Emotional numbness, or the inability to feel emotions, can also occur as a coping mechanism. Addressing these symptoms involves trauma-focused therapy and building a supportive therapeutic relationship.
- Self-Esteem and Identity Issues: Trafficking survivors often struggle with low self-esteem and a damaged sense of identity. Therapeutic interventions should focus on rebuilding self-worth, fostering a positive self-image, and helping survivors regain control over their lives.
- Substance Abuse: Many survivors use drugs or alcohol to cope with the trauma they have endured. Substance abuse treatment should be integrated into their overall care plan, addressing both the addiction and the underlying trauma.

Providing Comprehensive Care

- Holistic Assessment: Conduct a holistic assessment of the survivor's medical and psychological needs. This includes a thorough physical examination, mental health evaluation, and screening for substance abuse. Understanding the full scope of their needs allows for a more tailored and effective care plan.
- Trauma-Informed Care: Adopt a trauma-informed approach to care, which involves recognizing the prevalence of trauma and its impact on the survivor. This approach emphasizes safety, trustworthiness, and empowerment in the caregiving process.
- Integrated Services: Coordinate with other healthcare professionals and support services to provide comprehensive care. This may include referrals to mental

health specialists, social workers, legal advocates, and community organizations that offer additional support.

- Safety Planning: Develop a safety plan with the survivor to address immediate concerns and provide strategies for ensuring their protection. This may involve arranging secure housing, legal protection, or emergency resources.
- Empowerment and Autonomy: Empower survivors by involving them in their care decisions and respecting their autonomy. Providing information about their options and allowing them to make informed choices fosters a sense of control and agency.

Case Examples

To illustrate the application of comprehensive care, consider the following examples:

Case Example 1: A trafficking survivor presents with multiple untreated STIs and chronic pain. The healthcare provider conducts a thorough physical examination, treats the infections, and refers the survivor to a pain management specialist. The provider also offers counseling services to address the survivor's psychological trauma.

Case Example 2: An adolescent trafficking victim shows signs of severe depression and substance abuse. The healthcare provider coordinates with a mental health counselor and a substance abuse treatment program, while also addressing the victim's nutritional needs and providing resources for safe housing.

Addressing the medical and psychological trauma of trafficking survivors requires a comprehensive and compassionate approach. By understanding the specific health challenges faced by these individuals and providing holistic, trauma-informed care, healthcare providers can play a vital role in supporting their recovery and well-being. Effective treatment and support can significantly impact the survivor's ability to heal and rebuild their life, ultimately contributing to the broader effort to combat human sex trafficking.

MODULE FOUR

LESSON ONE: LEGAL AND ETHICAL CONSIDERATIONS IN CARING FOR TRAFFICKING VICTIMS

Healthcare providers play a critical role in identifying and assisting victims of human sex trafficking. However, this responsibility comes with complex legal and ethical challenges. This lesson explores the legal obligations and ethical considerations that healthcare providers must navigate when caring for trafficking victims. Understanding these aspects ensures that providers can offer compassionate and legally compliant care while safeguarding the rights and dignity of survivors.

Legal Obligations

Mandatory Reporting Laws: Many jurisdictions have mandatory reporting laws that require healthcare providers to report suspected cases of human trafficking or abuse to authorities. Providers must be familiar with their local reporting requirements, including what constitutes reasonable suspicion and the proper channels for reporting.

- Confidentiality and Privacy: Protecting patient confidentiality is a fundamental principle in healthcare. However, this can be complicated when reporting trafficking cases. Providers must balance the need to report suspected trafficking with their obligation to maintain patient confidentiality. Clear communication with patients about the limits of confidentiality is crucial.

- Informed Consent: Obtaining informed consent is essential in all medical interactions. Trafficking victims may be particularly vulnerable and may not fully understand their rights or the implications of medical procedures. Providers must ensure that patients are fully informed and voluntarily consent to treatment, without coercion.

- Legal Documentation and Testimony: In some cases, healthcare providers may be asked to provide documentation or testify in legal proceedings related to trafficking. Accurate and detailed medical records can be critical in legal cases, so providers must maintain meticulous documentation of all interactions and treatments.

Ethical Considerations

Autonomy and Empowerment: Respecting the autonomy of trafficking survivors is a key ethical principle. This involves supporting their right to make informed decisions about their care and respecting their choices, even if they choose not to disclose their trafficking situation or report to authorities.

- Non-Maleficence and Beneficence: Healthcare providers must prioritize the well-being of their patients, ensuring that their actions do no harm (non-maleficence) and actively contribute to the patient's health and recovery (beneficence). This includes providing trauma-informed care and avoiding actions that could retraumatize the victim.

- Justice and Equity: Ensuring that trafficking survivors receive fair and equitable care is essential. Providers must be aware of and address any biases or barriers that could affect the quality of care for trafficking victims. This includes advocating for access to resources and support services.

- Professional Boundaries: Maintaining professional boundaries is crucial when working with trafficking survivors. Providers must avoid becoming overly involved in the patient's personal life while still offering compassionate and supportive care. Boundaries help ensure that the care provided is professional and effective.

Navigating Conflicts

Balancing Reporting and Confidentiality: When mandatory reporting laws conflict with confidentiality obligations, providers must navigate these situations carefully. Discussing the reporting requirements with the patient and explaining the reasons for reporting can help maintain trust while fulfilling legal obligations.

- Handling Disclosures: When a patient discloses their trafficking situation, providers must respond with empathy and support while also considering the legal implications. Offering to connect the patient with legal and social services can help address their needs comprehensively.
- Ethical Dilemmas: Providers may face ethical dilemmas, such as when a patient refuses treatment or declines to report their trafficking situation. In these cases, providers should seek guidance from ethics committees or legal counsel to make informed decisions that prioritize the patient's best interests.

Case Studies

To illustrate the application of legal and ethical considerations, consider the following case studies:

Case Study 1: A healthcare provider suspects that a patient is a trafficking victim due to multiple untreated injuries and signs of control by an accompanying individual. The provider discusses the suspicion with the patient, explains the mandatory reporting laws, and assures the patient of their commitment to confidentiality and support. The provider reports the case while continuing to offer care and connecting the patient with support services.

Case Study 2: A young woman discloses to her healthcare provider that she is a trafficking victim but is afraid to report to the authorities due to threats from her trafficker. The provider respects her decision while offering resources for safety planning and connecting her with a legal advocate. The provider maintains detailed documentation of the interaction to support any future legal proceedings.

Developing Policies and Protocols

- Institutional Policies: Healthcare facilities should develop clear policies and protocols for handling suspected trafficking cases. These should include guidelines for reporting, maintaining confidentiality, and providing trauma-informed care.
- Staff Training: Ongoing training on legal and ethical issues related to trafficking is essential for all healthcare staff. This training should cover mandatory reporting laws, informed consent, and ethical principles in patient care.
- Collaboration with Legal Experts: Partnering with legal experts and organizations that specialize in trafficking can provide valuable guidance and support for healthcare providers. Legal experts can offer advice on complex cases and help develop effective protocols.

MODULE FIVE

LESSON ONE: MULTIDISCIPLINARY COLLABORATION: WORKING TOGETHER TO SUPPORT TRAFFICKING SURVIVORS

Effective support for trafficking survivors requires a multidisciplinary approach. Healthcare providers, social workers, legal professionals, law enforcement, and community organizations must collaborate to address the complex needs of trafficking victims. This lesson explores the importance of multidisciplinary collaboration, outlines the roles of various professionals, and provides strategies for effective teamwork to ensure comprehensive care and support for trafficking survivors.

The Importance of Multidisciplinary Collaboration

- Comprehensive Care: Trafficking survivors often have a wide range of needs that cannot be addressed by a single provider or organization. A multidisciplinary approach ensures that survivors receive comprehensive care, including medical treatment, mental health support, legal assistance, and social services.

- Holistic Support: Collaboration among different professionals allows for a holistic understanding of the survivor's situation. Each discipline brings unique expertise and perspectives, contributing to a more thorough assessment and tailored intervention plan.

- Resource Optimization: Pooling resources and knowledge from various sectors can enhance the effectiveness and efficiency of support services. This collaborative effort can prevent duplication of services and ensure that survivors receive timely and appropriate assistance.

Roles of Key Professionals

- Healthcare Providers: Medical professionals are often the first point of contact for trafficking survivors. Their role includes identifying potential victims, providing immediate medical care, conducting thorough health assessments, and referring patients to specialized services. They also play a critical role in documenting injuries and health conditions that may be used as evidence in legal cases.

- Mental Health Professionals: Psychologists, psychiatrists, and counselors provide essential mental health support for trafficking survivors. They address trauma-related conditions such as PTSD, depression, and anxiety through therapeutic interventions. Mental health professionals also help survivors build coping skills and resilience.

- Social Workers: Social workers provide case management and connect survivors with necessary resources, including housing, financial assistance, and educational opportunities. They also offer emotional support and advocacy, helping survivors navigate complex social service systems.

- Legal Professionals: Attorneys and legal advocates assist trafficking survivors with legal issues, such as obtaining legal status, pursuing justice against traffickers, and securing protection orders. Legal professionals also educate survivors about their rights and provide representation in court proceedings.

- Law Enforcement: Police and investigative agencies play a critical role in identifying traffickers, investigating trafficking cases, and ensuring the safety of survivors. Collaboration with law enforcement is essential for holding traffickers accountable and dismantling trafficking networks.

- Community Organizations: Non-governmental organizations (NGOs) and community groups offer a range of support services, including emergency shelters, job training programs, and peer support networks. These organizations often provide the ongoing support needed for survivors to rebuild their lives.

Strategies for Effective Collaboration

- Building Trust and Communication: Establishing trust and open communication among team members is fundamental for effective collaboration. Regular meetings, shared case conferences, and clear communication channels help maintain a coordinated approach to care.
- Developing Shared Goals: All team members should work towards common goals centered on the well-being and empowerment of trafficking survivors. Establishing shared objectives and clear roles can enhance teamwork and ensure that all aspects of the survivor's needs are addressed.
- Training and Education: Cross-disciplinary training helps team members understand the roles and expertise of other professionals involved in the care of trafficking survivors. Regular training sessions can improve collaboration and enhance the overall quality of support.
- Creating Comprehensive Care Plans: Developing individualized care plans that incorporate input from all relevant professionals ensures that survivors receive tailored and holistic support. These plans should be flexible and regularly reviewed to adapt to the changing needs of the survivor.

- Maintaining Confidentiality: Respecting the confidentiality of survivors is paramount. Clear protocols for information sharing should be established to protect the survivor's privacy while allowing for necessary communication among team members.
- Crisis Response and Safety Planning: Establishing protocols for crisis response and safety planning is crucial. Multidisciplinary teams should be prepared to respond to emergencies and ensure the safety of survivors, including creating plans for safe housing and emergency contacts.

Multidisciplinary collaboration is essential for providing comprehensive and effective support to trafficking survivors. By working together, healthcare providers, social workers, legal professionals, law enforcement, and community organizations can address the complex needs of survivors and facilitate their recovery and empowerment.

CONCLUSION

Human sex trafficking is a pervasive and insidious crime that exploits the most vulnerable individuals in society. As healthcare providers, we have a unique and critical role in identifying, supporting, and advocating for trafficking survivors. This book has explored the multifaceted aspects of human sex trafficking, from recognizing the signs and understanding the victims' experiences to providing comprehensive medical and psychological care and navigating the legal and ethical complexities involved.

The fight against human sex trafficking is a collective effort that requires the involvement of the entire healthcare community. Each provider, regardless of their role, can contribute to identifying victims, providing compassionate care, and advocating for systemic changes that protect the most vulnerable. Together, we can create a healthcare system that not only heals but also empowers survivors to reclaim their lives and futures.

The journey to eradicate human sex trafficking is long and challenging, but it is a journey that we must undertake with dedication and compassion. By equipping ourselves with knowledge, practicing trauma-informed care, collaborating with other professionals, and advocating for policy changes, we can be powerful allies in the fight against this heinous crime. Our actions can save lives, restore dignity, and pave the way for a future free from exploitation and abuse.

REFERENCES

- Baldwin, S. B., Eisenman, D. P., Sayles, J. N., Ryan, G., & Chuang, K. S. (2011). *Identification of human trafficking victims in health care settings. Health and Human Rights.*
- Clawson, H. J., & Dutch, N. (2008). *Identifying victims of human trafficking: Inherent challenges and promising strategies from the field. U.S. Department of Health and Human Services.*
- Dovydaitis, T. (2010). *Human trafficking: The role of the health care provider. Journal of Midwifery & Women's Health.*
- Gerassi, L. (2015). *A heated debate: Theoretical perspectives of sexual exploitation and sex work. Journal of Sociology and Social Welfare.*
- Hardy, V., & Hitz, M. (2015). *Human trafficking: A call for heightened awareness and advocacy by mental health practitioners. Journal of Social, Behavioral, and Health Sciences.*
- Hodge, D. R. (2014). *Assisting victims of human trafficking: Strategies for faith-based providers. Social Work & Christianity.*
- Lederer, L. J., & Wetzel, C. A. (2014). *The health consequences of sex trafficking and their implications for identifying victims in healthcare facilities. Annals of Health Law.*
- Macy, R. J., & Johns, N. (2011). *Aftercare services for international sex trafficking survivors: Informing U.S. service and program development in an emerging practice area. Trauma, Violence, & Abuse.*